SKUNKS AND THEIR RELATIVES

Published by Creative Education, 123 South Broad Street, Mankato, Minnesota 56001

Printed by permission of Wildlife Education, Ltd.

Library of Congress Cataloging-in-Publication Data

Biel, Timothy L.
Skunks and their relatives / written by Timothy Levi Biel.
p. cm. — (Zoobooks)
Includes index.
Summary: Discusses that family of mammals that is made up of skunks, weasels, minks, badgers, otters, ferrets, wolverines, and martens.
ISBN 0-88682-779-5
1. Mustelidae—Juvenile literature. [1. Mustelidae.] I. Title II. Series: Zoo books (Mankato, Minn.)
QL737-C25B49 1996
599.74'447—dc20   95-45324   CIP AC

SKUNKS AND THEIR RELATIVES

Creative Education

Art Credits

Pages Eight and Nine: Chuck Ripper

Page Eight: Bottom, Lew Sadler

Page Nine: Top, Raul Espinoza

Pages Ten and Eleven: Chuck Ripper

Page Ten: Top, Graham Allen

Page Eleven: Top, Graham Allen

Pages Twelve and Thirteen: Chuck Ripper

Page Thirteen: Top, Graham Allen; **Middle,** Walter Stuart; **Bottom,** Graham Allen

Page Sixteen: Chuck Ripper; **Top,** Michael Woods; **Bottom,** Walter Stuart

Pages Eighteen and Nineteen: Chuck Ripper

Page Eighteen: Bottom, Graham Allen

Page Nineteen: Top, Graham Allen

Page Twenty: Chuck Ripper

Page Twenty-One: Top Left, Michael Woods; **Top Right,** Chuck Ripper; **Middle,** Michael Woods; **Bottom Left,** Michael Woods; **Bottom Right,** Walter Stuart

Photographic Credits

Front Cover: John Cancalosi (*DRK Photo*)

Pages Six and Seven: James R. Fisher (*Photo Researchers*)

Page Eight: Jane Burton (*Bruce Coleman, Inc.*)

Page Ten: Top, Rod Williams (*Bruce Coleman, Ltd.*); **Bottom,** Bob and Clara Calhoun (*Bruce Coleman, Ltd.*)

Page Eleven: Top, Kim Taylor (*Bruce Coleman, Ltd.*); **Middle Left,** Rick McIntyre (*Tom Stack & Associates*); **Middle Right,** Breck P. Kent (*Animals Animals*); **Bottom,** Breck P. Kent (*Animals Animals*)

Page Twelve: Tom A. Schneider

Page Thirteen: E.R. Degginger (*Bruce Coleman, Inc.*)

Pages Fourteen and Fifteen: Erwin and Peggy Bauer (*Bruce Coleman, Inc.*)

Page Seventeen: Top, Rod Allin (*Tom Stack & Associates*); **Bottom,** Ernest Wilkinson (*Animals Animals*)

Page Eighteen: Left, Tom McHugh (*Photo Researchers*); **Right,** Tom Brakefield (*Bruce Coleman, Inc.*)

Page Nineteen: Jack Couffer (*Bruce Coleman, Inc.*)

Page Twenty: Wayne Lankinen (*DRK Photo*)

Page Twenty-One: Left, Stouffer Productions (*Animals Animals*); **Right,** Jeff Foott (*Bruce Coleman, Ltd.*)

Pages Twenty-Two and Twenty-Three: Hans Reinhard (*Bruce Coleman, Inc.*)

Our Thanks To: Bernard Thornton (*Linden Artists Ltd.*); Pamela Stuart; Tom Clark; Ed Hamilton (*San Diego Bionomics*); Deanna Leonhardt; Gary Marshall (*Marshall Research Inc.*); Rod McPherson; Lynn Prather; Michaele Robinson (*San Diego Zoo Library*); Karen Napolilli

Cover Photo: Striped skunk

Contents

Skunks and their relatives make up a family of mammals known as the *mustelids*. Besides skunks, this family includes weasels, ferrets, minks, martens, badgers, wolverines, and otters.

People and other animals go out of their way to avoid skunks and most of the skunk's relatives. That's because these animals have a secret weapon. They produce a sticky, smelly liquid called *musk*. A single squirt of musk is all it takes to keep most animals from bothering them.

The name "mustelid" means "mouse catcher." And some members of this family have ideal bodies for hunting mice. For example, weasels and ferrets have short legs and long skinny bodies, so they can squeeze right inside a mouse's underground den. But skunks and many others in the mustelid family are *not* skinny little mouse catchers. In fact, there is a great variety of shapes and sizes in this family. This variety allows mustelids to live in many different places and hunt different kinds of prey.

These nuzzling river otters are like other otters. Their natural curiosity and high energy lead to a lot of playtime.

The body of a mustelid is built low to the ground. It has short legs and a long, flexible backbone. There are many variations of this basic design, from skinny weasels to stocky wolverines. But all are built for capturing prey and eating meat.

Many of them have incredibly slender bodies, like the mink featured on these pages. Such thin bodies are wonderful for turning and twisting through heavy brush, and even for swimming. But they don't hold heat well. This is why minks and other mustelids have some of the warmest, most luxurious fur coats in the entire animal kingdom.

The thick, shiny fur of a mink reflects almost every color you can imagine. The shine is caused by oils that make the fur waterproof.

MINK

Mustelids may be small, but they can hunt animals that are much bigger than they are. This is partly because they have very strong jaws and sharp teeth.

The jaws and skull of a mustelid are surrounded by extremely powerful muscles. This makes even small mustelids, like the mink, unbelievably strong. It can hold its jaws shut for a long time so that its prey cannot break loose.

Mustelids have long pointed *canine teeth* Ⓐ for grabbing their prey. And their sharp *cheek teeth* Ⓑ slice meat so that it can be swallowed.

Minks and other mustelids have a strange way of running. It is really more like jumping, but it gives them a long stride, despite their short legs.

First they push off with both back feet ①. Then they stretch out in midair, reaching forward as far as they can with their front legs ②.

As their front feet hit the ground, they arch their backs. This brings the hind legs as far forward as possible ③.

From this position, they are ready to leap again ④. And with every leap, they take full advantage of their long bodies.

Mustelids have the most flexible backbone of any mammal in the world. This allows them to bend and turn their bodies as though they were made of rubber.

Most mustelids eat a lot of food, but they don't get fat. This is because they are always on the go, so they use all the energy from the food they eat.

For their size, mustelids are probably the strongest of all mammals. As you see at left, the mink is practically *all* muscle.

Weasels are even skinnier than minks. Yet they are probably the most effective hunters in the mustelid family. And that's good, because they are also the hungriest. For their size, weasels eat more food than almost any other predator on earth.

In fact, if a weasel stops eating for very long, it will die. Like you, weasels get their energy from the food they eat. But they burn it much faster than you do. So weasels need a constant food supply. For example, it takes a human about two months to eat its weight in food. But a weasel has to eat its weight in food every single day!

This leaves these tiny animals little time to rest. Even when they aren't busy hunting, they are often busy avoiding bigger predators that may be hunting *them.* Fortunately, weasels have a good way to hide, as you can see below.

The least weasel usually hunts mice, but if it gets hungry enough, it may even attack a cottontail rabbit that is five or six times its own size.

LONG-TAILED WEASEL (SUMMER)

The color of the weasel's coat helps it hide. Weasels that live in cold climates change their fur color twice a year. For most of the year, the fur on their head and back is brown. This blends with the colors of the forest, and it helps the weasels hide from both predators and prey.

HOURS OF DAYLIGHT	NIGHTTIME

HOURS OF DAYLIGHT	NIGHTTIME

LONG-TAILED WEASEL (WINTER)

The fur color changes automatically. It is controlled by the amount of daylight per day. In the winter, when there are fewer hours of daylight, the weasel grows a white coat that blends with the snow. And in the spring, as the hours of daylight increase, it grows a new coat of brown fur.

10

A weasel cannot even sleep through the night without getting hungry. Fortunately, it has an excellent sense of smell, which helps it find prey in the dark.

LEAST WEASEL

Most weasels will eat anything they can find. But one close relative of the weasel, the black-footed ferret, depends almost entirely on one kind of prey. It only hunts prairie dogs, and it lives in abandoned prairie dog burrows. These prairie dogs often use an unusual method to combat ferrets. Working together, they can quickly fill up a ferret's burrow with dirt!

Weasels are fearless hunters. They sometimes enter the burrows of large, vicious rats and attack them. The short-tailed weasel at left is fighting one of the biggest and most dangerous rats of all, a Norway rat.

COYOTE

Weasels hunt many different kinds of prey. But there are also many different kinds of predators that eat weasels. And many times, when the weasel is looking for a meal, it becomes the meal for some other animal. A few animals that eat weasels are shown here.

BOBCAT

Coyotes and bobcats don't go looking for weasels. They hunt squirrels, mice, and other less vicious animals instead. But if they come upon a weasel, they will often capture it.

BARN OWL

Owls are probably the weasel's greatest enemies. At night these hunters can swoop down and grab a weasel before it has a chance to run away.

11

Skunks are no bigger than housecats. Yet mountain lions, wolves, and even bears run away when they see a skunk, because they don't want to get sprayed. To avoid being sprayed by a skunk, they have to stay a safe distance away. Skunks can spray their musk accurately at objects 15 feet away (4.6 meters)!

Many people think that skunks spray everything in sight. But actually, they do not like to spray their musk. So they use it only when necessary. Most often, these furry little black and white creatures are fun to watch—especially a family of skunks out for an evening walk, like the striped skunks below.

Musk is a skunk's only defense, and it doesn't have an endless supply. So the skunk only sprays if it has to.

①

Before it sprays, a skunk has several ways to warn an intruder. First, it stomps with its front feet and rakes the ground with its claws ①.

A mother skunk is a wonderful teacher. She teaches her young how to hunt and dig for food and how to defend themselves. Until they are about six months old, young skunks follow their mother in single file wherever she goes.

Baby skunks are born with their black and white hair. And they can spray their musk even before they learn to walk.

STRIPED SKUNK

12

If the first warning doesn't work, the skunk arches its back, hisses, and raises its tail ②. In this position, a black and white skunk is easy to see. Its raised tail is like a sign that means, "Stop! Think where you're going!"

②

For most skunks, the raised tail is its final warning. But a spotted skunk may give one more warning, as you see at right ③.

③ Before it sprays, this skunk may do a "handstand." But if you see a spotted skunk do this, don't wait around until it gets all its feet on the ground. It can spray while its back legs are in the air!

The musk is stored in two pouches beneath the mustelid's tail. The tips of these pouches are like nozzles on a tiny pair of hoses. The animal forces musk through the nozzles by tightening its muscles around the pouches. A skunk can even control these nozzles and aim them at targets near or far away.

HOODED SKUNK

Skunks usually don't move very fast. But when they need to be, they are quick enough to catch snakes. The hooded skunk shown below has cornered a gopher snake. Sometimes this species even kills rattlesnakes!

People have tried almost everything to get the skunk smell out of clothes, hair, and skin. Household bleach is the best thing to use on clothes. But no one has found a secret formula for things that can't be bleached, like hair or skin. Washing them with vinegar or tomato juice probably works the best.

13

These young river otters are only 12 weeks old.

Badgers are born to dig. They live in deep underground tunnels. And they hunt by breaking into the underground tunnels where other animals live.

When badgers are threatened by predators, they can quickly escape by digging a hole, climbing inside, and filling it up with dirt. Their short powerful legs and long sharp claws can rip through almost anything. People have even seen them working their way through blacktop pavement!

Badgers live in many different parts of the world, and they dig for different kinds of food. The African honey badger digs honeycombs out of tree hollows and rock crevices. To help it find the honeycombs, it often has special helpers, as you can see below.

EUROPEAN BADGER

LONG-TAILED WEASEL

All mustelids have long bodies and short legs. But some are thin and others are not. As you know, weasels have the skinniest bodies. And at the other extreme, badgers have the broadest and flattest bodies of all the mustelids.

African honey badgers and little honey guide birds offer a remarkable example of cooperation. When honey guides see a beehive, they fly off to "tell" a honey badger. They circle around the badger and chatter noisily until it follows them to the hive. The badger digs into the nest with its sharp claws and eats the honey. As a reward, the little birds get to eat what is left of the comb.

The badger's flat body is perfect for its way of life. Its body is so wide that a badger can use it to block the entrance to its den. And once it is set in this position, it can fight off almost any attacker. The badger even has folds of loose floppy skin on the sides of its body that make it hard for predators to hunt it. If a predator bites the badger, it may just get a mouthful of loose skin.

AMERICAN BADGER

A badger can dig faster with its paws than you can with a shovel. But that's because each paw has five sturdy claws that are shaped like shovels. A badger can dig with 20 shovels at once!

A mother badger takes good care of her young. She keeps the babies inside her den until they are about six weeks old. Then she may let the little badgers go outside to play. When the mother senses danger, she quickly pulls them back inside.

Badgers chase mice, gophers, and even rabbits into their burrows. But when a badger does this, it may accidentally help a coyote get a meal.

A rabbit's burrow usually has two entrances. So when a rabbit hears a badger breaking in, it goes out the other way.

Once in a while, a coyote will follow a badger as it hunts. And just when a rabbit seems to have escaped from the badger, there will be a coyote waiting for it.

17

Wolverines are the strongest mustelids. Some people even call them *skunk bears* because "they smell like skunks and are as strong as bears!" This is an exaggeration, of course, but wolverines look so mean and are so clever that trappers and outdoorsmen have nicknamed them "mountain devils."

The combination of strength, smell, and cunning has made wolverines very unpopular with some people. They cause a lot of mischief by stealing food from people and destroying their property. As you will see, there is a good reason why wolverines do these things. They are simply looking for food. They live in the far north, where food is very scarce. So they take it wherever they can find it.

WOLVERINE

Wolverines will eat anything that crosses their path. They may even hunt animals that are much larger than they are, or steal food from fierce predators.

To catch large animals, wolverines climb trees. When an animal passes underneath, the wolverine pounces on it and knocks it off its feet. Wolverines even hunt moose and caribou in this way!

The ferocious nature and strong smell of a wolverine are enough to make most large predators abandon their prey. Mountain lions, wolves, and even bears will leave their prey behind when a wolverine approaches.

PORCUPINE

A wolverine can eat almost anything. But there are a few exceptions. If it catches a porcupine and tries to eat it, the wolverine may swallow hundreds of porcupine quills. And this may kill it.

A wolverine is too small to eat a large animal in one meal, so it saves the leftover meat. To make sure another animal doesn't steal it, the wolverine sprays the meat with musk. Then it digs a hole and buries it.

Wolverines can make life miserable for trappers. The animals are clever enough to spring traps without getting caught in them.

A trapper returning to his cabin may find that a wolverine has broken in, ripped everything to shreds, and sprayed its horrible-smelling musk on anything it could not eat.

Trappers often hang food or bait in trees to keep animals from getting it. But this doesn't stop the wolverine!

WOLVERINE

Wolverines are superb trackers that will follow their prey almost anywhere. They climb trees, cross rivers, and go over mountains. They even follow their prey into dark places, like caves and hollow logs. And they will keep following an animal for days if they have to.

Wolverines are aggressive hunters, but they have never been known to attack people. Yet even the bravest person doesn't want to get too close to a wolverine. Its musk reeks like the musk of a skunk. And if the smell gets on your clothes or skin, it will linger for days.

19

Otters spend most of their time in the water. Their long, thin bodies are ideal for swimming. They have powerful tails to push them along. The webs on their hands and feet help them steer. And their thick fur coats keep them warm in cold water. One species of otter has the thickest fur of any animal on earth.

Most otters live in freshwater rivers, but there are some that live in the ocean too. Wherever they live, all otters love to play. They pass many hours frolicking and exploring their surroundings. This curiosity and love of games has made otters the most popular with people of all the mustelids.

River otters need long stretches of clean, open water. Unfortunately, as time goes by, more and more rivers are becoming polluted. This means there are fewer places for otters to live. So there are fewer otters left in the world.

River otters never seem to get enough mud sliding! They slide down steep riverbanks and dive headfirst into the water. Then they climb back up the riverbank and wait their turn to slide down again. They may keep this up for hours!

Otters often use their webbed feet like rudders to steer them as they swim.

Sea otters dive for abalone, sea urchins, and other shellfish. They usually find them at the bottom of the sea where there are large beds of seaweed growing ①.

The otter finds a shellfish and tucks it under its arm ②. Then it picks up a large, flat rock and carries both the rock and the shellfish back to the surface ③.

River otters move almost as well on land as they do in the water. Their long toes give them a good grip on the ground, so they can run quickly.

SEA OTTER

Once it reaches the surface, the sea otter floats on its back and sets the rock on its chest. Holding the shellfish in both hands, it smashes it against the rock until the shell breaks ④.

RIVER OTTER

Sea otters spend almost all of their time in the water. Their front paws have short, stubby fingers that make it awkward for them to move on land. But short fingers are perfect for swimming and scooping up shellfish.

A river otter has to be a fast swimmer in order to catch fish. But it has a favorite method for catching them. The otter chases the fish into shallow inlets where it can corner them ①.

When the otter is sure the fish cannot escape, it catches it in its mouth. Then it carries the fish up onto the bank and eats it ②.

Ⓐ

Ⓑ

Sea otters swim in deeper water than river otters do, so they use their tails differently. The sea otter's tail Ⓐ is broader and flatter than the river otter's Ⓑ. When it swims, the sea otter moves its tail up and down, like a dolphin. But the river otter moves its tail from side to side, like a fish.

21

The future of weasels and other mustelids is important to people. But most people probably don't believe it. They think that mustelids are little pests that we should get rid of. They wonder why we should protect weasels when they sneak into chicken coops and kill chickens. Why should we protect skunks when they invade our yards and spray their smelly musk? Why save badgers when they dig up good grazing land?

The truth is, these animals do far more good things for people than most of us know. As a group, mustelids kill more rodents than any other group of predators. If it weren't for weasels and some of their relatives, it would be much more difficult for people to control all the mice and rats in the world.

Yet people usually pay more attention to the "bad" things these animals do. But these things aren't bad from the point of view of the animals. For example, a weasel is born to hunt. And to survive in the wild, it has to take all the prey it can find. So if a weasel finds an unguarded chicken coop, it just follows its instincts.

For thousands of years, these instincts have been helping weasels survive. But now, more people than ever before are crowding into areas where weasels and other mustelids live. And instead of trying to find ways to share the land and its resources with wild animals, people are driving them away. Or if its fur is valued, people may trap the animal.

Because mustelids have some of the most beautiful fur coats on earth, people have been trapping them for centuries. In fact, much of North America was first explored by trappers looking for fur, and they gathered millions of mustelid furs. Before fur trapping was controlled, minks, martens, and otters were nearly driven to extinction.

Fortunately, trapping is now controlled. And the number of minks, martens, and sea otters in the wild is growing. But at the same time, these and other mustelids are facing new dangers. People have polluted rivers where minks and otters hunt. They have chopped down trees where martens make their homes. And while trying to control rodents, people have accidentally poisoned many weasels and ferrets. Black-footed ferrets and wolverines are already close to extinction. Unless we find better ways to share the earth with wildlife, many other mustelids could soon join them.

Martens look like weasels with long, bushy tails. But instead of running along the ground looking for mice, they dart over tree branches and hunt squirrels. The marten's long, bushy tail helps it balance as it scampers through the treetops. This is a beech marten, which occupies woodlands from Europe to central Asia.

Index